by *Nancy and Randall Faber*

A BASIC PIANO METHOD

CONTENTS

10 April 2008

The Juggler

Mauro Giuliani
(1781-1829, Italy)

Rather fast

4 *on* ___?

f*-*p *on repeat*

1 *on* ___?

> 2 eighth notes divided
> between the hands.

DISCOVERY

How many beats does this rhythm receive? ♩♫ = ____ beats ✓

Teacher Duet: (Student plays 1 octave higher)

R.H.

L.H.

mp*-*p *on repeat*

FF1

Rhino in the Mud

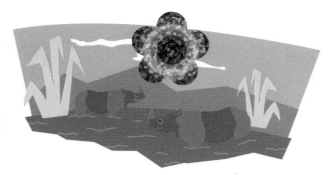

Notice the L.H. starts on the *lowest* G on the piano.

Very slowly

mf The rhino wallows happily in the mud.

Two rhinos wallow happily in the mud.

Two big rhi-nos *rit.* **roll in the mud!**

DISCOVERY Which measure has only eighth notes for the R.H.? *measure* ___

Home on the Range

American Folk Song

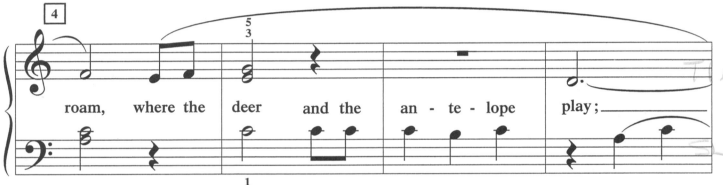

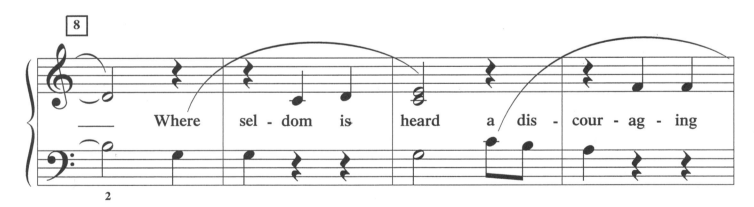

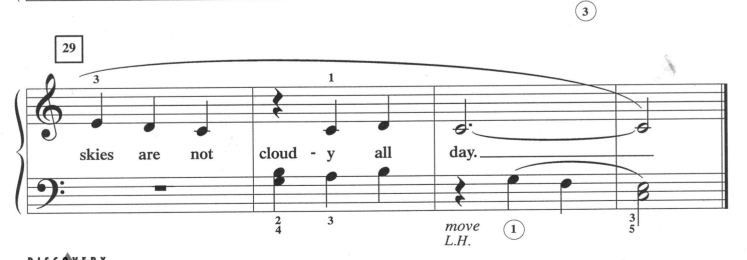

D I S C O V E R Y

In this piece, the 8th notes always fall on: (circle the correct answer)

beat 1   *beat 2*   *beat 3*

Theme and Variation

Name the 5-finger position. _____

S o u n d   C h e c k : Are you playing *legato* and *staccato*?

Theme

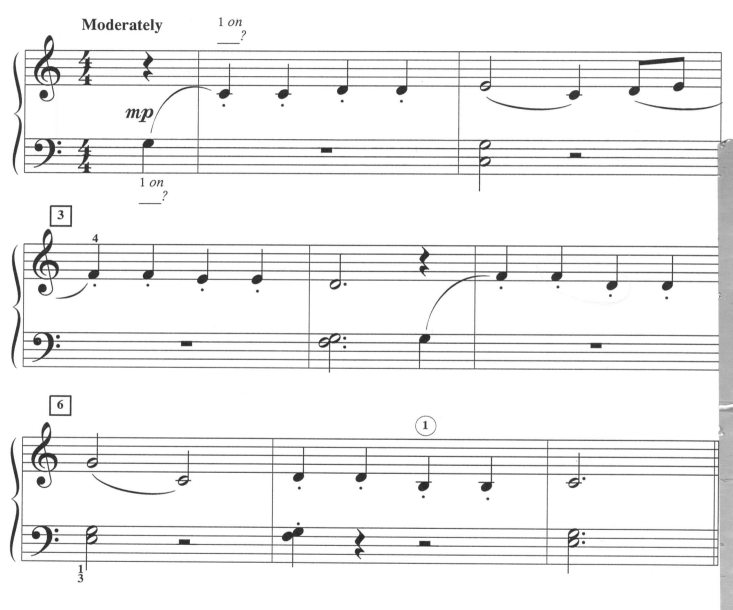

Teacher Duet: (Student plays 1 octave higher)

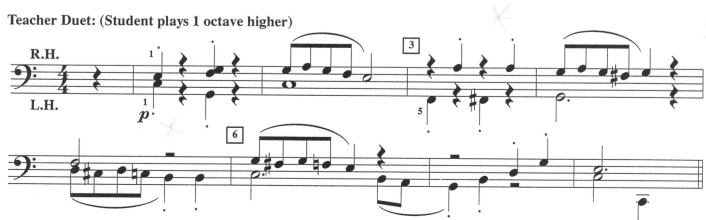

FF1

Variation

DISCOVERY Look at the variation. Is the *first* note of every measure the same as in the theme (p.6)?
(yes) / no (circle one)

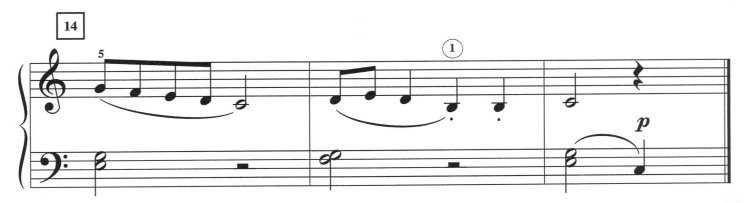

Green Frog Hop

Notice the different left hand position.

Lyric by Jennifer MacLean

With bounce

mf "Rib - bit   rib bit,   rib - bit,

1 on
____?   4   2

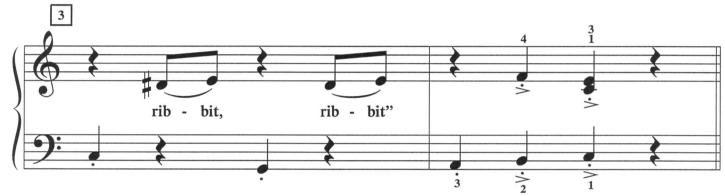

rib - bit,   rib - bit"

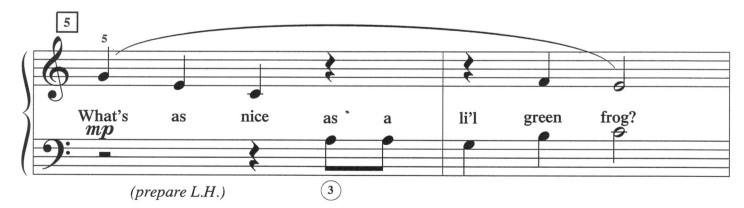

What's   as   nice   as   a   li'l   green   frog?

mp

(prepare L.H.)

It   won't   bark   like   a   big   old   dog.

FF10

9 Don't act mean like a cat up a tree, that's why it's al - ways a

12 frog for me! *mf* "Rib-bit, rib - bit rib - bit,

(prepare L.H.)

15 rib - bit, rib - bit!"

DISCOVERY

Point out the *natural* in this piece. Tell your teacher what it means.

Teacher Duet: (Student plays as written)

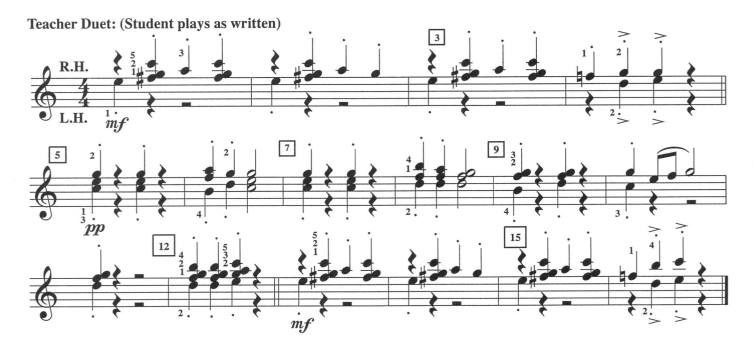

Road Runner

Name the 5-finger position. _____

Notice that both hands are written using the treble clef.

Running quickly

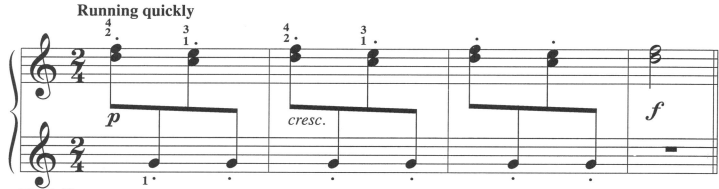

The L.H. starts
with 1 on the G
above Middle C.

Teacher Duet: (Student plays as written)

10

DISCOVERY

Is the L.H. starting note the *tonic* or the *dominant?* _____

Transpose this piece to G Position. What will be the new starting note for the L.H.? _____

Mr. McGill

Lively

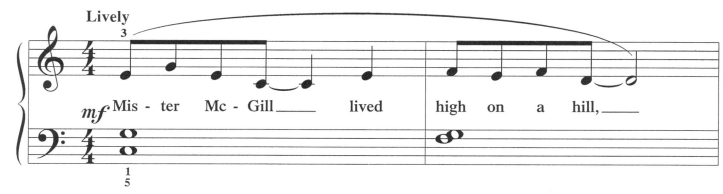

mf Mis - ter Mc - Gill____ lived | high on a hill,____

you can be sure that he | lives there still.____ | Ev - e - ry day____ the

neigh-bors all say,____ | he'd sing tunes at his pi - | a - no this way.____

L.H. moves quickly

"Doo - wah, doo - wah, | boop she - bop!____ | Boop she - bop!____

DISCOVERY

What is a phrase? Tell your teacher.

Point out at least four phrases in *Mr. McGill*.

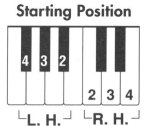

Starting Position

L. H. — R. H.

The Loch Ness Monster

Hold the right foot pedal down for the first 8 measures.

Words by Crystal Bowman

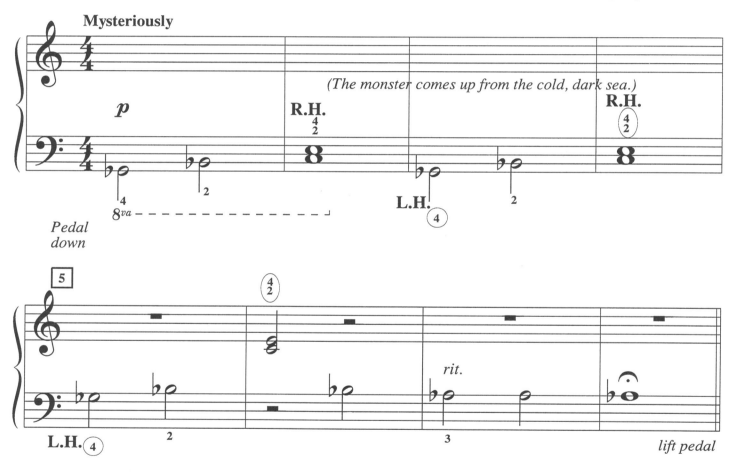

(The monster comes up from the cold, dark sea.)

Mysteriously

Pedal down

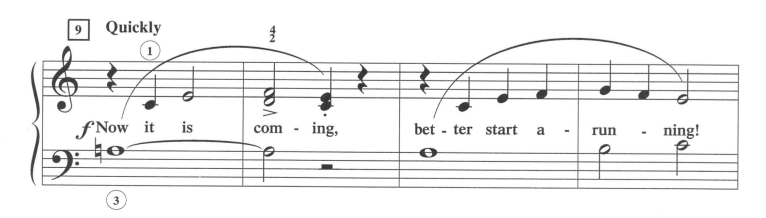

Quickly

f Now it is com - ing, bet - ter start a - run - ning!

FF101

March of the English Guard

D Position

Jeremiah Clarke
(1659-1707, England)

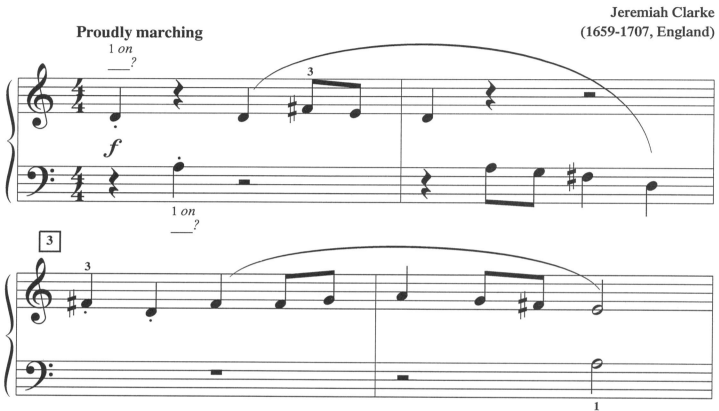

Proudly marching

Teacher Duet: (Student plays 1 octave higher)

FF10

DISCOVERY

What note is always played as a sharp in D Position? ____

Coconut Shuffle

Name the 5-finger position. _____

Note: The teacher may want to teach the rhythm in measure 1 by imitation.

Happily

Words by Crystal Bowman

mf Come and dance_ with me now, it's not hard_ to learn

1 on ___?
2 on ___?

how. Kick your feet_ so high, till they reach_ the sky,

Teacher Duet: (Student plays 1 octave higher)

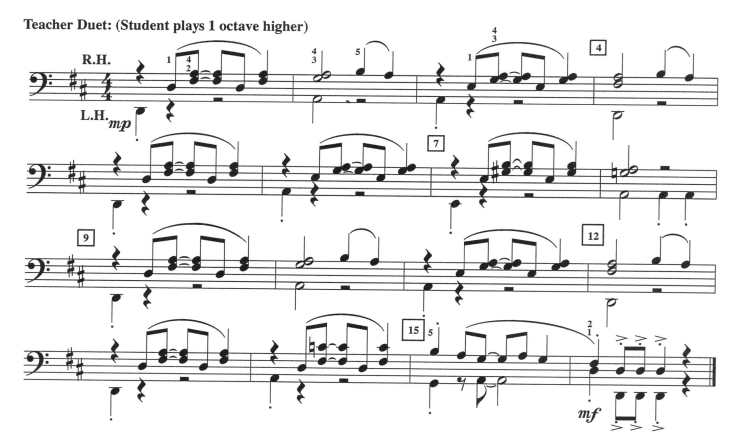

R.H.

L.H. *mp*

mf

18

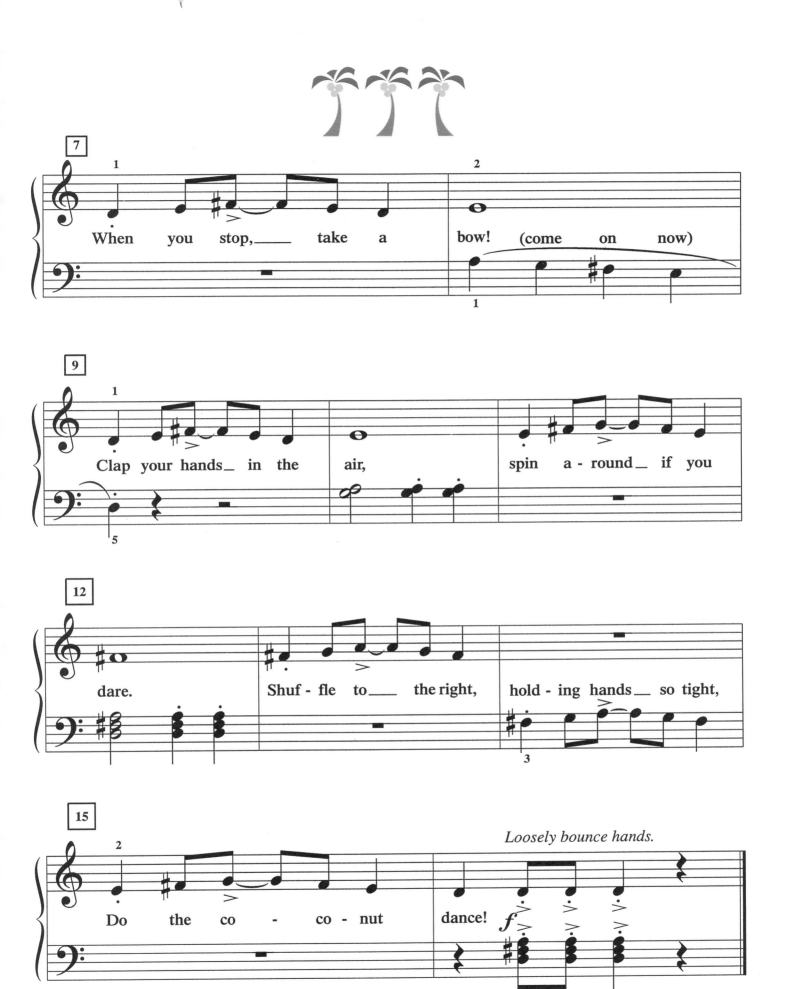

Rocky Mountain Train

A Position

FF10

DISCOVERY Where does the R.H. play a note that is *not* in the **A 5-finger position?**

Italian Children's Game

Name the 5-finger position. _____

Mauro Giuliani
(1781-1829, Italy)

Playfully, but not too fast

Teacher Duet: (Student plays as written)

FF1

Show your teacher four measures where the L.H. has the melody.

Then transpose *Italian Children's Game* to D Position.

Weeping Willow

D minor Position

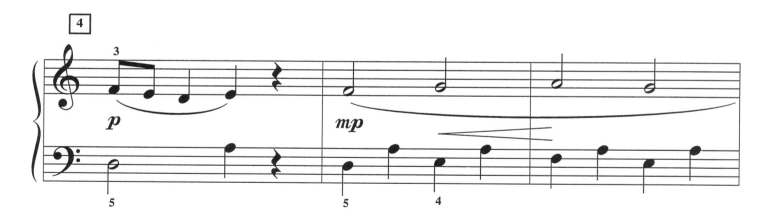

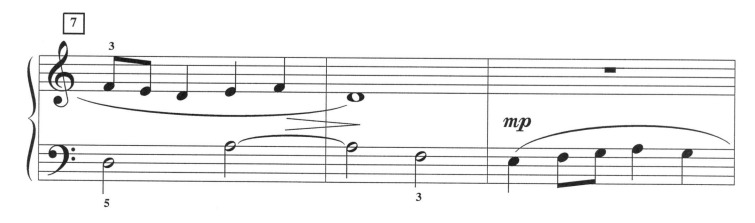

FF10

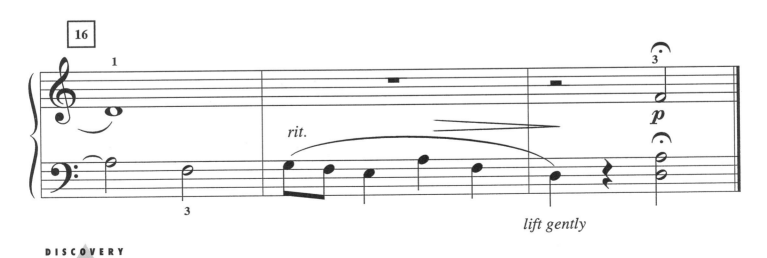

lift gently

DISCOVERY

Which note has to change to put this piece in D major position? ___

Duet playing: A *duet* is a piece for two performers.

Learn both the **Secondo** and **Primo** parts and play with another student (or your teacher).

Both duet parts are in **A minor Position.**

Building a Snow Fort

Secondo (second or lower part)

FF1

Building a Snow Fort

Primo (first or upper part)

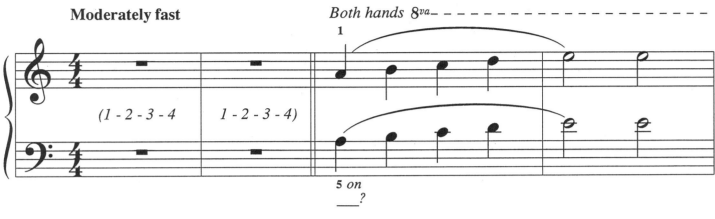

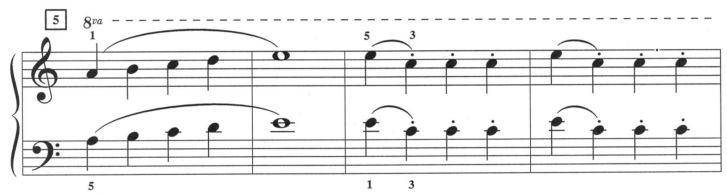

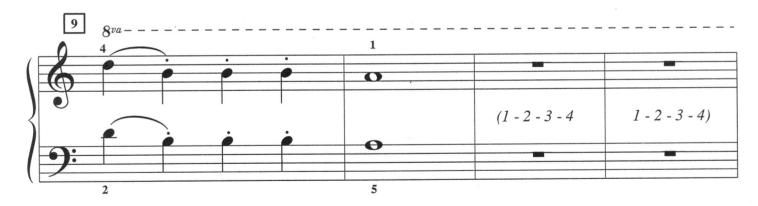

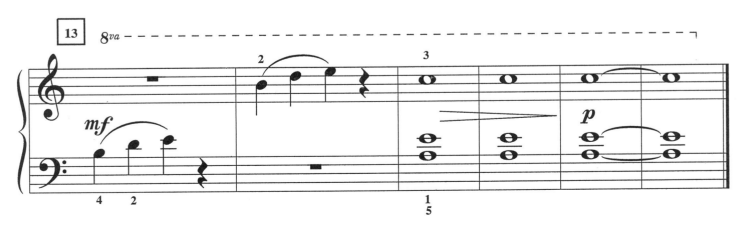

Practice this piece playing *andante* before trying the *allegro* tempo mark.

The Horseman's Night Ride

C minor Position

Teacher Duet: (Student plays 1 octave higher)

FF10

DISCOVERY How many beats does each whole rest receive in this piece? ___

Can you transpose *The Horseman's Night Ride* to G minor position?

Dance of the Irish

G minor Position

Allegro moderato (moderately fast)

1 *on* ___?
5 *on* ___?

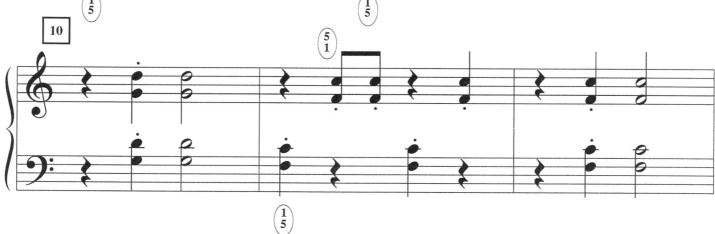

FF10

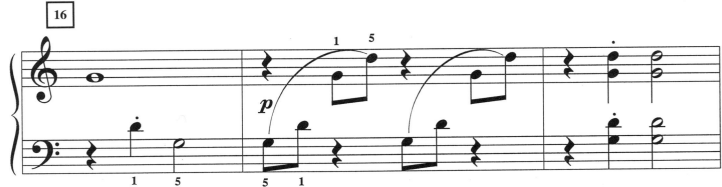

Move L.H. quickly
to Bass G Position.

DISCOVERY

This piece has a special ending added. Tell your teacher where you think the ending section begins.

FF1